this is how you live

a book of poetry

RACHEL TOALSON

Other Books by Rachel

Poetry

this is how you know
Life: a definition of terms
The Book of Uncommon Hours: haiku poetry
Textbook of an Ordinary Life

Essay

Parenthood: Has Anyone Seen My Sanity?
The Life-Changing Madness of Tidying Up After Children
This Life With Boys
We Count it All Joy: Essays
Hills I'll Probably Lie Down On

To see all the books Rachel has written, please click or visit the link below:

www.racheltoalson.com/writing

this is how you
live

Published by
Batlee Press
Post Office Box 591596
San Antonio, TX 78259

Copyright ©2019 by Rachel Toalson
All rights reserved.
Printed in the United States of America.
Interior design by Toalson Media.
Cover design by Ben Toalson. www.toalsonmarketing.com

No part of this book may be reproduced or transmitted in any form or by any means, electronic or mechanical, including photocopying and recording, or by any information storage and retrieval system, without permission in writing from the publisher. For information regarding permission, write to Batlee Press, PO Box 591596, San Antonio, TX 78259.

The author appreciates your taking the time to read her work. Please consider leaving a review wherever you bought it and telling your friends how much you enjoyed it. Both of those help get the book into the hands of new readers, which is incredibly important for authors. Thank you for your support.
www.racheltoalson.com

Names: Toalson, Rachel, author.
Title: This is how you live / Rachel Toalson
Description: First edition. | Batlee Press, Texas:
Batlee Press Books, 2019

10 9 8 7 6 5 4 3 2 1

First Edition—2019

For C.C.
and all those who, like me,
wrestle with brain disorders
and the judgment of others
that inevitably follows diagnoses
remember you are loved
even when you have lost your mind

Introduction

It was a strange year.

You would think that the year you see one of your biggest dreams come true—which was, for me, the publishing of my first traditionally-published book—you would not be able to contain the joy and satisfaction and pleasure you took from life.

Instead, I found myself tail-spinning into a season of depression. I launched my book out into the world, did author appearances and signings, taught kids writing at several schools, played the part I needed to play—but even during what would seem to anyone else like a victorious accomplishment, I could feel my smile slipping. I grasped at joy, at prayer and meditation, at rest—anything I could find, but I know how depression works; I've wrestled with it for most of my life.

For me depression tangles around anxiety and obsessive-compulsive tendencies—including but not limited to anorexic thoughts and sometimes even behaviors, all in addition to the unexplainable sadness one might expect with depression and the mostly latent anger one wouldn't know to expect with depression unless one had experienced it.

Most depressive seasons I endure what I know will eventually pass by writing, almost obsessively, as though it can save my life (and maybe it does). This depression was different. Perhaps because it hit me during the vulnerable time when a book I'd spent years writing and perfecting released into the world, or perhaps for another reason entirely, I could not write. All the projects I'd been working on—and there were several—ground almost to a halt. Instead of using my work time to write I wanted to sleep or escape the world by reading or sit in my gray-blue wing chair, pretending I was invisible. This lack of desire to write—which had never ever been a part of the equation—scared me. I thought this depression might be the one that broke me.

And then one day, as I stared at my notebook, I started a poem about the fact that I could not write and ended it with "this is how you know it will be bad." And it was as though the words were waiting for permission. They spilled out onto the page, arranging themselves into poetry (as is often the case when I find myself at the bottom of the world). I wrote about my depression, my fears, my worries, my anxiety, my thoughts about myself and my body. I didn't hold back—because sometimes the best thing we can do for ourselves is tell the truth.

After we sink and sleep, I hope we will always find the strength to rise—and if we can't, I hope others in our life will help us with that rising. It is what I pray for every person who reads this book.

sink

1.

one little thing goes wrong
one little change to the schedule
one little deviation in the
structured plan

>and you're falling into the pit
>scraping against the sides
>hoping you won't go as
>far down as last time

this is how
you sink

2.

turn it around
get out of bed
stop crying
don't be so sensitive
they'll all think you're crazy
maybe you are
stand up stand up stand up
why are you so weak
so many have it worse than you do
what if you screw them up
it's the best time of the year—
    so why can't you be happy
chill out
it's not that bad
shut up
you have nothing to contribute
they'd probably be happier
    without you
nobody wants to hear
    your sob story
forget about it—
    it was a long time ago
grow a thicker skin
practice more self-control
well you really messed up that one

you'll never get off the ground
    with that attitude
don't you ever stop worrying
get control of yourself

this is how
you flog yourself

3.

you see her
at the monthly meeting

she's wasting away
but instead of feeling alarmed

you feel jealous
you would like that wasting-away body

instead of this
large and disappointing one

so you make your plan
steel your courage

take a breath as though it can
sustain you through the starving

and you pass on
supper

this is how
you let anorexia reclaim you

4.

you play the chameleon

you've done it all your life
tried to be less of a burden
tried to smile when you felt
    more like crying
tried to shape yourself into
whatever the situation demanded
tried to insist
    you don't need help
    you can handle it yourself
    things are just fine

the lies rolled
off your tongue
like hollow pearls

you're so good at it
they can't even tell
what game you're playing

and to be honest
neither can you

this is how

you lose yourself

5.

you stare at the blank page

the words are
    gone
    vanished
    nonexistent

you don't even have
a desire to write
and you've never not had
a desire to write
you take every moment
you can to write
now you have a moment and

    you can't write

this is how
you know it will be bad

6.

You had one mole
that needed a more
invasive removal of its
atypical cells.
You visit the dermatologist
every six months now.

You examine your moles
every couple of days
    Has that one grown larger?
    Is that a new one?
    Should you be worried?

The answer is, of course, *Yes*.

This is how
you drive yourself crazy.

7.

You are familiar with the ways
some of them think
    it's all in your control
    the darkness represents
        a failure in your life
    you've been melodramatic
        as long as they've known you
    there are always worse circumstances
        than your own but some people
            (meaning you)
    cry over spilled milk.

Sometimes you accidentally
let their voices too far
inside.

This is how
you forget it's not your fault.

8.

So much to do,
    hurry hurry hurry
send that email
watch him play
hardly hear the commentary
from the one who wants to talk
watch the minutes
plan your time
spend every moment
in a rush to make it to
your own personally decided
finish line—
which continues to get
    farther away.

This is how
you let life pass you by.

9.

She calls,
says there's nothing wrong
with the ovaries but
the endometrium is thickened.
She throws out some medical jargon.
You feel the familiar cold and then
the heat blasting your face and neck.
She recommends followup with a gynecologist.

You hang up,
pull up the Internet,
research every medical term
she threw out so nonchalantly,
almost glibly,
with an obsessiveness
that speaks of a will to live,
a need to understand,
a pulsing hope to be reassured.

It's much worse
than you thought.

This is how
you lose a day to worry.

10.

the school counselor calls
says he mentioned he
wants to kill himself
you cry on the other end of the line
doesn't he know
how much he is loved?
you know this isn't
how it works but the words
sweep in anyway

he's your son he's your son he's your son

she says, *we'll work
on a plan of
treatment and prevention*

you say: *yes
we will too*

and when you hang up
your mind endlessly worries
the question:
how might you have been
a better mother so
he wouldn't feel this way?

because the world
likes to point fingers
and sometimes you
accidentally believe them

this is how
you give guilt a foothold.

11.

you interviewed
some suicidal teenagers
for a book you wrote
one of them said

> *I don't want to have kids*
> *I would never want*
> *to pass along my*
> *mental illnesses to them*

it's not until later
that you wonder:
is this what you've
done?

this is how
you give guilt a stronger foothold

12.

All day you've been thinking about
that one unsubscribe on your email.
It was your stepmother.
She marked your newsletter
as having spammy content,
after (you think) reading
a short essay about
your dad leaving your mom
and the way you grew up
without any child support from him.
Maybe she doesn't want to
face up to the facts.
Or maybe it was
a mistake on her part.

> you let it eat away at you
> you let it tell a story of
> your competence or lack thereof
> you let it silence you

This is how
you stumble.

13.

You had to miss the holiday party.
Life has been overwhelming lately,
and the idea of staying two days
away from home is
a little too much to ask.
He says he understands,
but does he really?

Does he know that playing a part
sends you deeper into the hole

that shoving away this
all-consuming worry
enough to have a conversation
is currently impossible

that fielding questions of "How are you"
ignite your anxiety because your words
are slippery and unpredictable things
and the phrase "I'm doing well, thank you"
might trade places with
the silent "I think I'm depressed"
clanging in your head

Maybe he's noticed

your silence.

As soon as he's gone,
you regret not going
you should have gone
you should have been
     strong enough to handle it
look what you're doing to your family
why can't you just be happy

This is how
you punish yourself.

14.

pinch
pull
turn around,
glare at yourself
    with that practiced eye
    the one that says
    what a shame
    it would be to be

seen

this is how
you unlove yourself

15.

sometimes you let
a thought snake in:
They leave because of me

>your father
>a best friend
>your partner will be next— you're sure of it

so you stack another stone
on the leaning walls
around your heart

this is how
you stay safe

16.

When you were a kid
you watched *The Goonies* and
sat in the bathroom thinking
about how everyone, one day,
becomes nothing more than a skeleton.

You cried,
bit your fingernails,
tried to come to terms with it.

You could say
you've always had a
preoccupation with dying,
an existential predisposition
to pondering the end of things.

You try to forget
    that phone call from your doctor
    all there is to be afraid of
    all that could hasten death
but tonight it's impossible.

This is how
you crash and burn.

17.

Don't get so stressed, he says,
like it's something that is simple,
and for him, it is.

You stress
    because you care
    because it's important
    because if you don't—who will?

This is how
you explain your sinking.

18.

you go in for a Pap smear
like you do every year
thinking this one will be like
all the others

except it's not
your doctor calls and says
the results were abnormal
you'll have to get more testing done

she sighs, either weary
because this happens all the time
or sad because it doesn't and
now it's happened to you

you look up all the possibilities
let them crowd your mind
until you can't
think straight

this is how
you lose a week.

19.

He says
> *Sometimes I can't breathe
> like the back of my throat
> closes up.*

You think
> *I know what that is.*

You think
> *Anxiety plagues him, too?*

You think
> *My God, have I done this
> to all of them?*

This is how
you welcome guilt.

20.

When he takes
all the kids with him
the worries mount—

> what if something happens
> what if there's an accident
> what if you lose them all—

that's it
you're afraid of losing them all
you don't want to even think

what if what if what if what if what if

This is how
you get trapped in the spiral.

21.

the fog hangs over your head
pressing between your eyebrows

he asks you
what you think

you're not sure—no really
you're not sure what you think

he thinks it's an excuse
to give a non-answer

but truly it's too hard
to do something as simple as

think about what it means
that your son's

getting behavior notes
sent home

can't you just
get some sleep?

this is how

you know you're sinking

22.

it's the time of year
when you're supposed to be
carefree and happy

you don't feel much of anything
you make excuses—
it's a busy time
there's so much on your plate
maybe it's from last year's trauma
when your brother was diagnosed
with brain cancer

maybe there are
a hundred reasons
maybe there is only one

the beast has a name
but you don't ever call its name—
it calls yours

this is how
you keep sinking

23.

How are you? she asks.
You haven't seen her in a while
don't even really know her that well
and all you have to do is keep it together
    just keep it together

what happens when you
can't keep it together?

Maybe it's been too long since
you were honest with anyone
    especially yourself.
Maybe it's time.
Maybe this is not the place,
but you can't stop the words:
I feel like things are falling apart
and what you mean is
I feel like I am falling apart.

You don't know what
she'll do with your admission.
She looks a little surprised.
Maybe you've scared her.
But then she says
We all feel like that sometimes don't we?

And they're just simple words
but they mean everything because

this is how
you remember you're not alone.

sleep

24.

what's for dinner
is the kind of question
that can send you into
        a panic attack

because you hadn't really
thought about it,
hadn't thought at all beyond this
        one moment in time

where you are suspended
in a frozen pond
weighing a thousand
        pounds

it's clear that life goes on beyond
the murky ice block, you could never
forget that, they would never
        permit you to forget that

but that you are a part of it
        life
feels surprising
inconceivable

the simplest of things
are rendered impossible
when your body is made of
    concrete

what's for dinner
you wish you knew
you lie on the floor
    and stare at the ceiling

and pretend the
question they asked
did not breach your
    meditative concentration

This is how
you freeze

25.

You haven't heard
from them in a while.
You know they're questioning,
wondering about you.
You feel every misstep and
wonder if you have to hide it,
to spare them,
to spare yourself from them,
because you know what they'll think
if you give so much as a hint
that you've fallen into
the hole again.

They'll point to your faith,
say, *She just needs more Jesus*,
question whether you even believed
in the first place,
think what a shame it is
that you've lost the way.

So you don't reach out,
don't tell,
don't open up.
Some things are worth
holding close to yourself.

This is how
you protect your heart in the hole.

26.

Every time you look in the mirror
you have to turn away.

Every time you stand up
you want to quit eating.

Every time you feel
your stomach rumble

you remember why
you can't answer the call.

This is how
you torture yourself.

27.

Do you want to go? he says.
You hesitate for a minute. *No*, you say.

because you need time alone
because it would require too much energy
because maybe it would be
just enough to send you
over the edge

everything feels fragile now
so you curl up
lock the doors
keep yourself safe

this is how
you isolate

28.

He says *I feel like I just want to die.*

You think *How can he say that?*
You think *Haven't I loved him enough?*
You think *Where did we go so wrong?*

You think *What if?*

This is how
you falter.

29.

You're in a doctor's office.
She points to the place
on the boxes where
you've checked yes,
you struggle with
anxiety and depression.
No box exists for former anorexic.

She says, *Do you
take any medicine
for that?*

No, you say.
*I'm afraid it will
interfere with my creativity.*

What do you do? she says.

I'm a writer, you say.
She nods like she understands.

You've been asking
the question for a while:
can't have one without
the other, can you?

This is how
you justify.

30.

you are worried about
creativity

you're also worried about
the money it would take
to keep you on medication

you're worried about
    your wellbeing
    their understanding
    your future
    your mind
    your hope

the worries sometimes
swallow you up

you sometimes
let them

this is how
you fall victim to the cycle

31.

your son sings a song
at his choir concert
and in the middle of it
you find you're weeping
you put on your sunglasses
so he won't see
so the ones around you won't see
so the whole world won't see

this is how
you play the part

32.

You read a book about how
scientists postulate that
        depression
results from a mind that
can't stop thinking about itself,
over and over and over in a cycle
that won't quiet.

They say it's a cycle,
you liken it to a spiral.

The mind must be jolted
out of its rigid thinking, they say,
for a person to break free of
        depression.

You think that sounds
about right.
You wonder how
to jolt your mind
out of its rigid thinking

but it probably wouldn't
work for you
so why try?

This is how
you let negativity win

33.

he can't find his wallet

you go over the possibilities—
        where he went
        what he did
        why

the places it might have been
        left behind
        stolen
        dropped by a loose-fitting pocket

like
        the parking lot
        the store counter
        the box he opened yesterday

all day he looks
it had cash in it
you'll probably never see it again
someone will have a grand Christmas now

by the end of the day
the hope you felt upon
seeing the sunrise on your

walk to your sons' school this morning

will shrink too small to feel anymore

this is how
you let a day beat you

34.

Why is Mama crying again?
one of your sons says.

You turn your face away.

    again
    again
    again
it seems the most
frequently repeated question
in this season is
    why is Mama crying
    why is Mama crying
    why is Mama crying
Sometimes you don't even know
but of course you can't
tell them that.

You're afraid it will scare them.
You're afraid you are doing
irreparable harm to them.
You're afraid the instability of
not being able to pinpoint
why Mama is crying will do
lasting work on them.

They watch you closely.
You say, *I'm just sad about something.*
You blink your tears away
swallow hard
try to eat the rest of
your dinner.

This is how
you construct an alternate reality for your kids.

35.

the words come out softly at first:
sometimes I feel sad about things

then a little louder
one of them looks at you

What things?
he says

Everything, you say, *and nothing
sometimes there's just sadness*

They're quiet around the table
for half a second before

they return to pontificating
about their days

This is how
you name reality to your kids

36.

He bought a treadmill today.

Money's been tight,
so you can feel the pinch
in your shoulders.
You're not sure it will be okay;
the future assures nothing and
there are needs that require money,
needs that make this purchase of want
feel frivolous.

It was a Christmas present, he says.

But the worry remains,
like a snake hissing in the background:
What if?
The panic rises,
hot, then cold,
an arm goes numb,
you feel like you're dying,
your breath catches
then it's over
but not really.
Never really.
The shockwaves

stretch into future moments
you can't see from here.

But you try to smile.
You're not sure you succeed.

This is how
you ruin a perfectly good gift.

37.

you grew up thinking
this was a failure
on your part
they didn't have to tell you

it was braided into all their words
like a punch intended to
keep you wondering
if your faith was too small

some days you still wonder
and the wondering makes you cold
and the cold makes you tired
and the tired makes you climb back in bed

this is how
you succumb to the ghosts of the past

38.

You could try it maybe
    It probably wouldn't work

But maybe it would.
    You don't have the energy

But wouldn't it be worth the energy?
    You might not get out of this

You will. You've done it before
    But this one's worse

Is it?
Or is that just the imagination?

This is how
you wrestle with doubt

39.

I'm sorry
you find yourself
saying more often.
It's because you're emotional,
you cry at the least little thing,
your kids are looking at you
with those worried faces.
You apologize because you
feel guilty for worrying them.
You apologize because you
think you shouldn't be crying.
You apologize because you
believe that's what they need.

They don't.
All they need is yourself,
    all of it,
right now in this moment.
All they need is to feel
the never-ending
warmth of love,
still settling around them,
and even tears cannot carry
that away.

This is how
you love in spite of melancholy.

40.

tuck up your corners,
don't say a word about
the darkness that stalks you
pretend there is absolutely
nothing you can't handle

you are just fine
you are just fine
you are just fine

this is how
you protect yourself

41.

it doesn't happen all the time
maybe that's what makes it endurable
or maybe that's what
makes it so surprising
when you're lying in bed
about to drift off to sleep and
something wraps around
your neck and starts squeezing—
    that bill you got in the mail
    the well being of your children
    a deadline coming up at work—

and your right side
goes hot then cold
then you can't feel it at all
maybe you're having
a stroke or a heart attack
maybe you're dying
do they know
    without a doubt
how very much you love them
your life passes before you
but it's not like they say
    a montage of
        happy-moment pictures

it's more like a
disappointing diagnosis
stamped upon your years
and regret hits like
a cold splash of surf

and then it's over
you open your eyes
you're alive and
he's sleeping beside you
warming your back

this is how
you survive an anxiety attack

42.

Ninety percent of my time is spent
dealing with the crises of my kids, she says.

You say, *don't*
I know how that goes.
I have one in counseling
for suicidal depression,
one worried about speech lessons
and dealing with anxiety,
two in the middle of testing
for attention deficit and hyperactivity disorder
and various processing disorders.
I feel guilty all the time when I work
because they need so much from me.
But I also know who I am
without my work.

She says, *We should talk more.*
Help each other through the hard times.

This is how
you feel less alone.

43.

when he turns on
the music or
bangs it on the piano
close your eyes
and let the notes swell
like staccato strings of
        hope

you'll take all you can

this is how
you endure

44.

You don't like to be alone.
So when he says, *I'll take them all
to the church*, you almost say
you'll come, too.
But not going would
give you hours of alone time,
during which you could
get so much done,
uninterrupted by
needs and wants.
You could take a break.
Focus.
Finish that project.
Read.

You wrestle back and forth:
What if something happened?
What if having you there in the car
keeps him awake and alert?
What if you are the magic piece?

Are you the magic piece?
Maybe.
Probably not.

But you let him go,
watch him pack them all in the car,
wave goodbye and let them
travel those roads without you,
and the silence, you find,
doesn't feel scary.
It feels comfortable,
an invitation to breathe.

And you think, *maybe*

this is how
you take a breath.

45.

at the bottom
you remind yourself
there are

        one in four people in the world

living with brain disorders
and mental illness

this is how
you remember you're not the only one

46.

you don't want to
get out of bed
you don't actually
know if you can
The world is
too heavy right now
you've curled up under its cover
so you can feel alive with
the heat of your own body
because as soon as you
leave this space
you know you'll freeze
again

he says, *they'll understand
if you can't make it*

you say, *will they?*

of course
but you're not so sure
and the guilt comes sliding in
through the rents of the dark
and you wonder if you'll
ever be able to hold

your head high again

a message pings
from another friend
*so grateful for you and
your words*, she says

does she know their cost?
don't dwell on that
instead let the words sink in
let them speak long after
the lights turn off
let them proclaim
what you've wondered
all along

this is how
you remember you matter

47.

They say
God never gives you
more than you
can handle.

They say
it will all
work out.

They say
you'll see.

You know they mean well.
So you don't remind them
that life isn't always a neat
little tied-up box.
But you know and remember
and bow your head to pray
the only prayer that will
come freely anymore:
Help.

This is how
you keep holding on.

48.

you know there is
        beauty
in the world

you know there is
        joy
you know there is

hope wonder
        truth
security strength courage

bliss
        love
you know that you will

experience the
        fullness
of the world again

this is how
you conquer a moment

49.

the music twirls
around the room

and you realize
for the first time

in a long time
you want to dance too

this is how
you awaken

50.

One day you walk downstairs
on your way to the kitchen
        to refill water
        make some tea
        grab something from the fridge
        wash dishes
it doesn't matter.

What matters is:
you're singing.

This is how
you know you're on your way out.

rise

51.

lie on your floor
feel the rub of the carpet
on your back
the warmth of your legs
pressed together
the pulse of your heartbeat
coursing through your body
hear the birds outside
singing a song you remember

you are alive
and this is a brand new day

this is how
you find yourself again

52.

admit you're not okay
admit you're overwhelmed
admit you're not sure you can handle it
admit you're not sure you even want to try
admit you haven't been sleeping
admit you've been sleeping too much
      at the wrong times
admit you sometimes feel helpless
admit you don't know what to do
admit you need help

this is how
you climb from the pit

53.

You made a list for this book.
You remembered instances
where you worried,
things that happened,
circumstances that knocked
you down flat.
And you felt the
quickening of your heart,
the anxiety that remains
ever-ready to visit,
sliding in without your invitation,
at the mere mention of
a list.

But you tell yourself the truth:
       You are strong.
       You are courageous.
       You are held.

This is how
you overcome.

54.

Life doesn't always
make the least bit of sense.
Sometimes you can predict
how your efforts will go,
sometimes you're surprised
by an unexpected word or
gesture or look and
your whole world turns
on a fidget spinner before
coming to rest in a place that looks
both like and unlike where
you were standing moments ago,
a place that is the same but
>   brighter
>   clearer
>   lovelier

The hole fills up
the clouds burn away
the sea calms

You never know
when it will get better;
you may as well stick around
for when it does

This is how
you keep holding on.

55.

You put your head on his chest,
play the Sleeping Game.
You really are feeling sleepy.
He giggles.
You pretend to startle awake.
He laughs even harder.
You do it again.
This time you laugh along with him.

Do it again and again and again
until a three-year-old's joy and mirth
feels contagious.

This is how
you let the sunshine in.

56.

i

    you think
maybe he's like this
because I did
something wrong

    you think,
I wish I'd known
all my problems
before I had kids

    you think
I never meant
to pass this
along

ii

    you think
I only did the best
I could do

    you think
maybe that's
enough

you think
at least he knows
he's loved

this is how
you forgive yourself

57.

He pulls you into an embrace.

    He says, *Do you feel how our bodies fit together?*

    He says, *Do you want to see what I see?*

He turns you around to the mirror.

    He says, *Look.*

You don't want to, you don't want to, you don't want to—

    He says, *Open your eyes.*

Gentle words that peel your lids.

You see the same old body that started this in the first place.

    He says, *Say it.*

    I am beautiful, you say.

It doesn't matter if you don't believe it today.

Say it again tomorrow.

And the next day and the day after that, until

    this is how
    you let no eating disorder claim you

58.

Sit in a bright white room.
Talk about your fears,
your slight pain,
your wasted day.
Let her words climb down
to the deepest places:
As far as she can see,
you're perfectly healthy.

Remember it
for the next time
(there will be a next time).

This is how
you reclaim a day to hope.

59.

They make it sound so easy—
    cast your cares
    there is no fear in love
    perfect love casts out fear
    be not afraid

pray pray pray pray pray pray pray

You've always wanted
an easy solution,
but you know by now
there's not one.

You wish you could tell your mind
to do what they advise,
but a mind sometimes has
a mind of its own and
    besides
not much important is solved
by simple solutions.

So let the pressure off.
Stop trying to be what they
expect you to be.
Find your own way.

Your vices
don't diminish your
worth.

This is how
you set aside simple solutions.

60.

remember who you are
remember what is true
remember how desperately
        the world needs your words and
        you

this is how
you catch yourself in the stumble

61.

learn a new vocabulary:
        I am beautiful

learn to look at yourself with
        compassion and love

learn to let yourself eat without
        guilt sidling up too close

learn to take it
        one day one hour one moment at a time

it will take work—
        maybe years but

this is how
you free yourself

62.

Count the calories if you must,
but don't let it become an obsession.

Immerse yourself in the workout,
but do it because it makes you feel good,
not because you want to look a certain way.

Cover up because it's cold,
not because you don't want to be seen.

This is how
you know it's real.

63.

Try on that new outfit.
Look in the mirror
without analyzing all the
familiar flaws.
Instead, appreciate
the way that wine color
accentuates your eyes.

This is how
you take one step toward loving yourself.

64.

You know this
does not define you.
You know it does not
change who you are.
You know you are just as
        significant
        worthy
        beloved
as you ever were.

You know it does not mean
you are broken beyond repair—
is anyone, really?

You remind yourself
        again and
        again and
        again.

This is how
you stand strong against misunderstanding.

65.

You're afraid you'll be alone
You're afraid it's too hard
You're afraid it will demand
        your life
        your love
        your self

But you do it anyway—
        square your shoulders
        lift your head
        boldly speak your truth

And you find
        once out there
others like you

This is how
you brave the wilderness

66.

Spend a minute
       every day
    speaking truth
    imparting wisdom
    practicing a gentle humanity
    and compassionate radical empathy

This is how
you seize a life.

67.

check in
open up
let them see the real you
even though others in your past
abandoned you

tell them what you need
share what's in your head
          however fearful
let their acceptance
curve around you like
a tent in still wind

the ones who matter
will stay

this is how
you really stay safe

68.

the wind bends trees;
how much more
will it bend you?

the wind twirls leaves;
how much harder
will it twirl you?

the wind rips off roofs;
how much longer before
it rips off yours?

but trees straighten
leaves come to rest
roofs can be repaired:

remember

this is how
you know you'll survive

69.

You lie on the floor,
back pressed to the carpet,
legs stretched out in front of you,
eyes closed.

In the darkness
you see words,
folded into balloons:
    the names of your sons,
    your brother,
    money,
    the latest project
        you're working on,
    what you look like,
    money again—

You watch the balloons
float away into
a cloudless sky,
worries lost to
a distant horizon.

This is how
you seize a day.

70.

not everyone understands depression

some will say you should
- pray more
- take every thought captive
- get Jesus
- take your medicine
- suck it up
- get over it—they did
- stop dwelling
- don't worry so much
- practice gratefulness
- fix your thoughts on what is good
- take a walk
- get out of your head
- count your blessings
- try harder

they mostly mean well

smile
hold your head high
and walk away when
the solutions swell
too large to contain

and don't give
their diminishing guilt
a stronghold.

remind yourself
as often as it takes:

not everyone understands depression

this is how
you take care of yourself

71.

say the words
over and over and over again
however long you need:

>   I'm not broken

I am
    remarkable
    unusual
    spectacular
        me

this is how
you love yourself

72.

They used to sterilize
people with brain disorders.
Before that
       and sometimes simultaneously
they would euthanize them
as though this were a
life unworthy of life.

You know better.
But you like to compare
what happened then,
when mental illness was
       intolerable
       inconceivable
       misunderstood
to what happens now,
when mental illness is
       on the cusp of
       scientific understanding
       and acceptance.

This is how
you remember how far we've come.

73.

Embrace your mistakes
and all your intricacies,
including the neuroses.

Banish shame in favor of
worth and love.
Stop being so hard on yourself

and remember:
we're all human—
bound by love, hope, and error.

This is how
you reject the pressure to be perfect.

74.

What is it to you
what they think?

They can call you weak,
say you're making
a big deal out of nothing,
tell you the world's full of hard knocks
and others have endured them
much better than this.

Remember their words
don't change who you are.
Remember they have no power
over you unless you allow them power.
Remember that brave doesn't mean
> hiding
> pretending
> denying.

This is how
you stand.

75.

sometimes your alarm
will go off in the morning
and you don't want to
get out of bed and
you have so much to do
that won't get done unless
you get out of bed and
you will lie there guilting yourself
for feeling too tired
        too down
to climb out of bed
when you're supposed to
climb out of bed

        stay in bed
        close your eyes
        go back to sleep

sometimes we need more rest
before we face the day

this is how
you fight the monster strong

76.

Can you afford it?

What this question does to you
is difficult to explain.
Trauma wraps around it,
wraps around you,
so every purchase feels like
another step closer to the
dark hole of need.

What lies at the bottom
of the hole?
You're sure it's disaster.
You brace yourself.

But it turns out
it's just another pit
out of which
you learn to climb.

This is how
you meet fear head on.

77.

for so long
they've told you who to be:

>   don't take it too personally
>   don't cry too much
>   don't dwell on it
>   don't worry be happy
>   keep it all inside under cover
>   don't talk about it
>   stop crying
>   be quiet
>   go outside and play
>   put down that book
>   put down that pen
>   get out of your head
>   listen to me
>   maybe lose some weight

today you shrug off those expectations
like a fleece coat you've been wearing
for too many summers

this is how
you shed the weight of expectation

78.

Tell someone.

This is how
you really protect yourself.

79.

Don't let them
make you feel wrong
for the decisions you make about
    your kids
    your partner
    your career
    your spiritual understanding
    your life
The ones judging you
are working with a
limited understanding of
    who you are

Remember who you are—
    it's not who they say you are

You have
    nothing to justify
    nothing to explain
    nothing for which to apologize
Hold your head high
look them in the eye
and live your life

This is how

you belong to yourself

80.

Tonight there was a twitter chat.
You joined because
    it's the final one of the year

because
    you missed the last few for
    a non-expiring unannounced
    social media hiatus

because
    you think it might be
    good for you.

But you notice not many see you.
You notice they don't really respond.
You notice it's as though you don't exist.
You wonder why you even bothered.

And then you remember:
your vision's been crooked
all day.

This is how
you change your lenses.

81.

They want you to be
>someone you're not.

It's okay to tell them,
>*This is who I am*
>*and I am worthy of love.*

This is how
>you fight for yourself.

82.

You ran four miles today
You can feel your old self
peeking around the clouds
You wonder if it's too soon
to tell

Keep running
Step into those shoes
you used to wear
lift your head
set your rhythm
feel the breath heave
in and out of your chest
and let yourself believe
this is enough for

    today

This is how
you fly

83.

one day at a time
one hour at a time
one minute at a time

opening yourself
to love and
be loved

accepting and acknowledging
your dignity and
worth

silencing the negative
thoughts and voices that try
to tell you who are you and who to be

focusing on what is
good honorable lovely
true—yes especially true

this is how
you heal

84.

You think,
*I might not be all right,
but I'll be okay.*

You think,
*I've been here
before.*

You think,
*Remember what happened
then?*

You pick up
your journal.
You write.

This is how
you let the past work for you.

85.

let the storm rage
let the dark night come
let the winds whip
the hairs of your head
and upend your feet from their
carefully controlled spot

and then stand up again

this is how
you keep swinging

86.

Today the mom of your son's friend
comes over to ask about something
and you end up talking for hours about
> depression
> mental illness
> children
> spirituality
> parenting
> how to turn the tide
>> on toxic masculinity.

You open up and
she meets you and
you wonder why
you waited so long to
compare notes.

At the close of the conversation
you exchange numbers
and you know you've made
a new friend.

This is how
you build a community of like-minded people.

87.

They will tell you
    in no uncertain words
who they think you should be
    to ensure the fullness of this life
    to ensure you will receive a treasure later
    (because that will only happen their way)
    to ensure you will inherit the promise
    made smaller by their limited imaginations

They will tell you
    how you should write
    what you should do
    the ways you are wrong
and you will see it all written
clearly on their faces:
    they don't believe you've considered
    the repercussions of what you do

They will
    discredit you
    wipe your words from their slate
        of worthy reading material
    let their certainty speak for
        your uncertainty
    question whether you are

>   who you say you are

And you will falter in the moment—
you will
> defend
> admonish
> forget for the barest bit
>> who you are

And then you will
listen to the one
> who carries all authority
> who has the last word
> who knows you
>> completely and definitively

And you will remember:
> beloved
> worthy
> wondrous
> covered
> held
> justified

This is how
you remember who you are

88.

the morning is only
   dark
for a moment

do you see the
   sun
blinking over the horizon

let its golden
   fingers
stroke your face

feel its
   warmth
ease into your frozen places

smell its
   promise
on the breath of a new day

this is how
you rise again

89.

the spiral sweeps you into
the middle of the bottomless ocean

you breathe
    one two three
    hold release again

the gloomy thoughts
clutter

you imagine traps
    snagging them
    carrying them into oblivion

The night gets
too dark

you turn on
    the light.

This is how
you survive.

90.

Today you go for another run.

The miles slip away
and with them
    the worries
    the fears
    the darkness that has
    dimmed the world's brilliance.

By the time you are finished
your heart has jump-started,
the air feels invigorating,
the sky has turned a brilliant pink
that no words can describe
and when your son asks you
what color it is
you can only reply that
it's the color of
        hope.

This is
how you win.

91.

Shake off the things they say,
the words you think wait
between the lines.

Learn to move with the waves,
wading in the shallow end barefoot,
treading water in the deep end,
holding your breath for the moments
the wave drags you down.

Don't try to fight it coming,
it's important to conserve energy,
move where the current takes you,
keeping your own terms.

I am strong, I am courageous,
I am kind, I am loved:
a chant, on repeat.

And another:
    I will survive this.

You almost drowned
in the ocean once,
but you have practice

swimming underwater now.

So swim.

This is how
you live.

the end

About the Author

Rachel is the author of four poetry books, *This is How You Know*, *Life: a definition of terms*, *The Book of Uncommon Hours*, and *Textbook of an Ordinary Life*, and a middle grade novel in verse, *The Colors of the Rain*. She has been writing poetry since the time she could hold a pencil and form what passed for letters on the page. Her first introduction to poetry was the brilliance of Shel Silverstein, whom she still reads today. She recently exposed her sons to the hilarious Jack Prelutsky poem, "Homework! Oh Homework!" which was one of her favorites as a kid. They loved it (as she still does).

Her poems for children and adults can be read in literary magazines and online publications around the world.

Rachel lives with her husband and six sons in San Antonio, Texas. She daily reads poetry (as well as many, many books) to her children, because poetry, she says, contains the essence of life, and reading, she says, is the gateway to a future of promise.

Author's Note

My dear reader,

We are living in an age where mental illness is more widely understood than it used to be. But there are still misconceptions that abound, shame braided into diagnoses, and a stigma that those who suffer carry around with them. It keeps them quiet about their disorders, keeps them questioning their worth, keeps them wondering if a diagnosis tells the whole story of who they are.

We are so much more than a diagnosis that comes around a few times every year or that visits us every day.

One in four people in the world live with a brain disorder (brain disorder is, I think, a better term for it than "mental illness," which implies that there is a cure; those of us who live with brain disorders know most can't be cured, only managed). There are a lot of us out there, and I hope that if you are a person without a brain disorder this book has shown you a little glimpse of what it's like to live with one—though I must say, emphatically, that I don't speak for all those who wrestle with clinical depression, anxiety, and obsessive-compulsive disorder; we are all as different as our personalities. This is a peek into one life touched by brain disorders.

If you are a person with a brain disorder, I hope you have found within these pages encouragement in your identity, a reinforcement of your hope, and a reminder that you are more than your disorder, that you are brave and spectacular and deserving of every good thing that comes your way. I hope, when you forget how very much you are loved, you will open this book again and remember.

Stay strong, keep swimming, and reach for the light.

In love,
Rachel

Acknowledgments

How would I stand without my community of people behind me? I am so grateful to:

Ben, who pulls me through so much, holds me when there are no words, and loves me in spite of all my failures.

My sons—Jadon, Asa, Hosea, Zadok, Boaz, and Asher. Thank you for your patience, for the blazing light you bring to this life, for the hard conversations you have so willingly and the hugs you launch at me so frequently. I'm sorry some—or all—of you will struggle, too, but I am trying to provide for you a good example for how to manage your disorders. Thank you for loving me even when I don't.

My community of like-minded people—you know who you are.

The poets who cut a path before me by saying it was okay to write about brain disorders.

Mom, who passed along to me these disorders (maybe only half) but who remains a constant in my healing because of the way she loves.

God, who holds on when my grip slips.

Enjoy more titles from Rachel Toalson

racheltoalson.com

Rachel Toalson Poetry
Starter Library

Enjoy more of Rachel Toalson's poetry with these free downloads.

To get your FREE books, visit *
RachelToalson.com/FreeBook

*Must be 13 or older to be eligible

www.ingramcontent.com/pod-product-compliance
Lightning Source LLC
Chambersburg PA
CBHW030118100526
44591CB00009B/440